You are valuable!
Jon Enochs
10-22-2022

Copyright © 2022 Joan Enockson

All rights reserved. This book, or any parts, may not be reproduced in any form without written permission from the publisher.

"Millie Mammoth" is a work of fiction. This story is original and all characters are products of the author's imagination. Any correlations to real life are purely coincidental.

ISBN: 9781958023167 (Hard Cover)
ISBN: 9781958023174 (Paperback)
ISBN: 9781958023181 (eBook)

Library of Congress Control Number: 2022913928

Cover design by Joan Enockson
Illustrations by Joan Enockson
Graphics purchased for commercial use from Fairy Tale Photo Edits

JUV001000, JUV002120, JUV002140, JUV019000, JUV051000, JUV039060, JUV039090, JUV039140

First printing, 2022

Joan Enockson
Tall Girl Publishing
Laurens, IA

joanenockson.com
joanenockson6@gmail.com

This book belongs to:

_____

A gift from:

_____

Millie Mammoth

Dedication

- This book is dedicated to my sons, Lucas and Ethan, who wisely chose good friends and continue to do so. I am so proud of them!

Way up north
in a land of snow and ice,

there lived a woolly mammoth,
who loved to play with mice.

No one in her life truly understood,

when Millie took her tiny friends to play in the woods.

There was Betty, Shirley, Mike, and Fred,

who climbed up her trunk
to ride on her head.

"Millie," they cried, "run fast through the snow!"

"Alright," Millie said, "hold tight, don't let go!"

Snow flew to the left, and then to the right.

With each tree they passed the mice squeaked with delight!

They raced up a hill, and followed a trail.

Saw a big log,
and over they sailed!

When all of a sudden, Millie fell flat!

Her foot, she saw, was caught in a trap.

"Can you help me?" cried Millie, her eyes filled with hope.

"My foot is all tangled up in a rope."

Betty, Shirley, Mike and Fred, saw it was just as Millie had said.

They chewed through the ropes until nothing was left.

"Thank you!" cried Millie,
"You mice are the best!"

The mice climbed back up to the top of her head.

"I'm so happy to have you as friends," Millie said.

They made their way back through the woods and the snow.

This time more slowly, due to Millie's sore toe.

Her family and friends saw Millie in pain,

and glared at the mice,
wanting someone to blame.

"Oh, no!" Millie cried, understanding their thoughts.

The leader of the mammoths stepped forward to speak.

The mice sat frozen, not daring to squeak.

"But you are welcome here as friends we can trust."

As each face relaxed and the truth sunk in,

they all thought it nice
to have mice as friends.

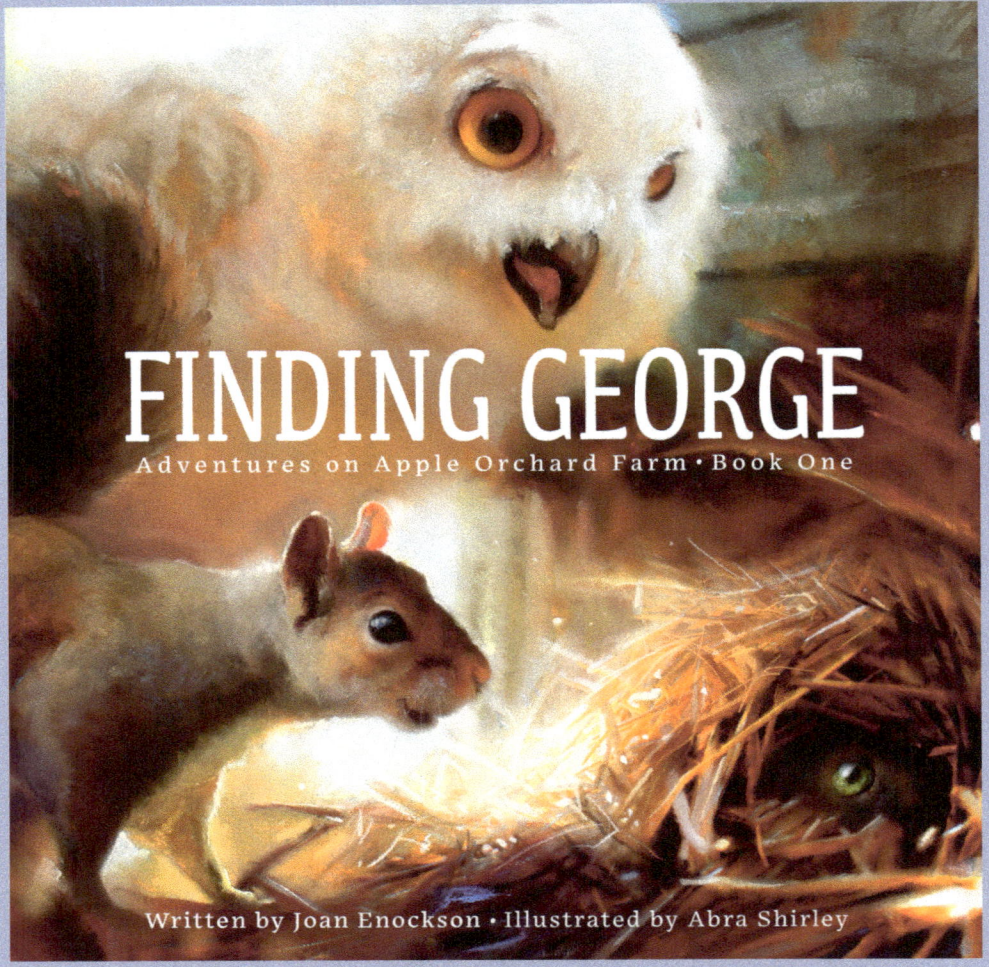

Late at night Orville hears noises, but he can't identify them. He recruits his best friend, Simon, to help investigate and solve the mystery. They are surprised at what they find!

This touching story introduces the first set of characters in Book One of the *Adventures on Apple Orchard Farm* series. This series focuses on the social-emotional needs of children and the skills necessary to develop healthy relationships. "Finding George" includes characters who show empathy for the negative effects of bullying as well as the emotional challenges of living with a disability.

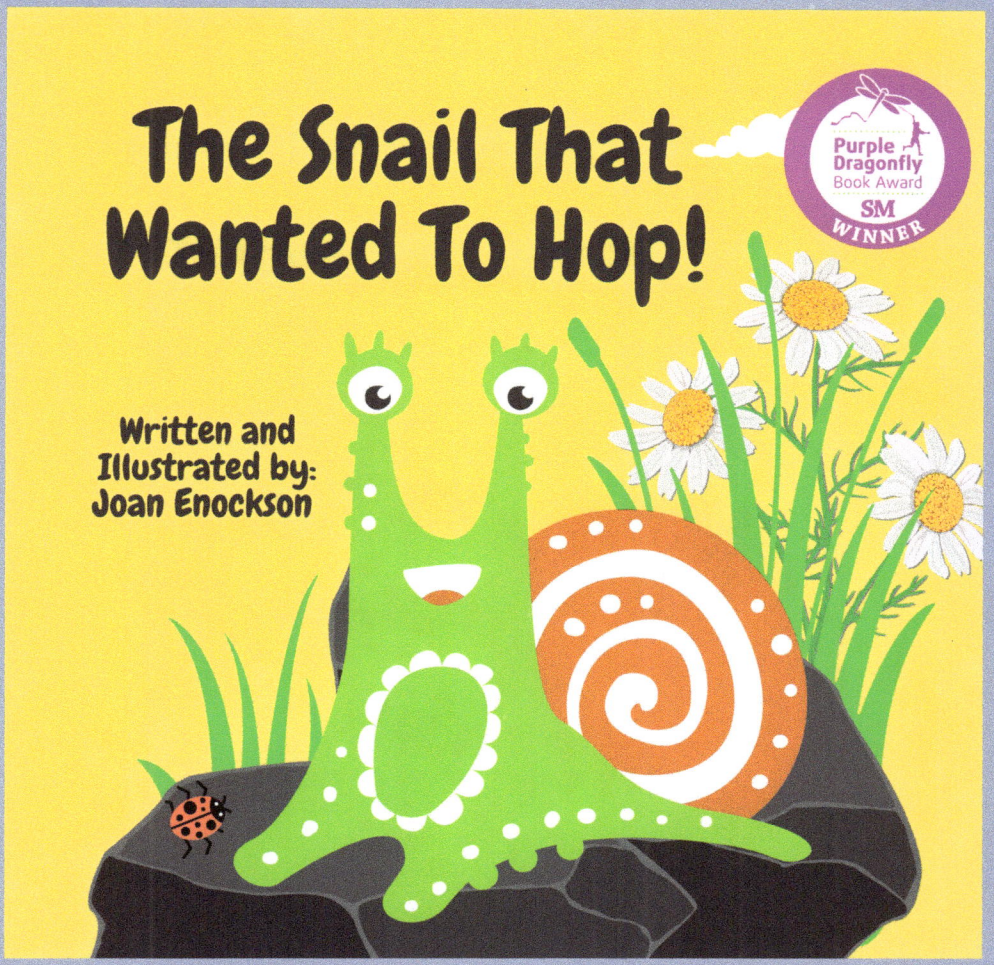

Sid the snail wants to hop! He sees others hopping and wishes he could do the same.

This is a delightful story about a snail who dreamed big, tried many times and failed, problem-solved with the help of a new friend, and overcame his obstacles.

Lili wants to earn money! With the help of her grandparents, neighborhood friends, and her older brother, Lilli learns the value of hard work, support, and good business practices to build a successful business.

Joan Enockson is an educator, musician, and author of children's books.

Her books address social-emotional needs, friendship, citizenship, and patriotism.

She has experience teaching children of all ages in the public school system, and strives to write in a style that intrigues young readers.

joanenockson.com
joanenockson6@gmail.com

CPSIA information can be obtained
at www.ICGtesting.com
Printed in the USA
JSHW062326230922
30960JS00001B/2